World of Insects

Ants

by Deirdre A. Prischmann

Consultant:
Gary A. Dunn, MS, Director of Education
Young Entomologists' Society Inc.
Lansing, Michigan

Capstone press

Mankato, Minnesota

Bridgestone Books are published by Capstone Press,
151 Good Counsel Drive, P.O. Box 669, Mankato, Minnesota 56002.
www.capstonepress.com

Library of Congress Cataloging-in-Publication Data
Prischmann, Deirdre A.
　　Ants / by Deirdre A. Prischmann.
　　　p. cm.—(Bridgestone Books. World of insects)
　　Includes bibliographical references and index.
　　ISBN 0-7368-3705-1 (hardcover)
　　1. Ants—Juvenile literature. I. Title. II. Series: World of insects.
QL568.F7P65 2005
595.79'6—dc22   2004014837

Summary: A brief introduction to ants, discussing their characteristics, habitat, life cycle, and predators.
Includes a range map, life cycle illustration, and amazing facts.

Editorial Credits
Becky Viaene, editor; Jennifer Bergstrom, designer; Erin Scott, Wylde Hare Creative, illustrator;
　　Jo Miller, photo researcher; Scott Thoms, photo editor

Photo Credits
BrandX Pictures, back cover
Bruce Coleman Inc./George D. Dodge & Dale R. Thompson, front cover; J. C. Carton, 12;
　　Kim Taylor, 4, 10
Digital Vision, 1
James P. Rowan, 18
Pete Carmichael, 6, 20
Rob Curtis, 16

1 2 3 4 5 6 10 09 08 07 06 05

Table of Contents

Ants

Have you ever been to a picnic? Did you see small insects eating food? Were they walking in lines? Those insects were ants. At least 10,000 types of ants live in the world.

Ants are insects related to bees and wasps. Insects have six legs, three body sections, and an **exoskeleton**. An exoskeleton is a hard outer covering. It protects an insect's body.

◄ Ants are usually seen in large groups, like these green tree ants.

What Ants Look Like

An ant's body is divided into three sections. These sections are the **thorax**, **abdomen**, and head.

Ants have three pairs of jointed legs on their thorax. A narrow waist connects the thorax and abdomen.

An ant's head has eyes, **antennas**, and mouthparts. Ants feel and smell with their antennas. They use their mouthparts for fighting and eating. Mouthparts are also used to dig tunnels.

◄ The bullet ant is known for its painful sting and large body size. It can be 1 inch (2.5 centimeters) long.

Ant Range Map

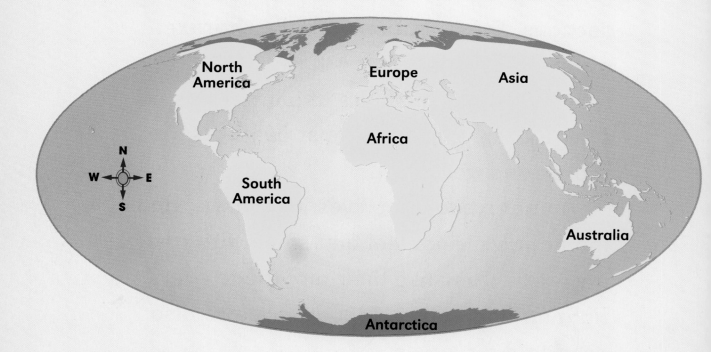

North America

Europe

Asia

Africa

South America

Australia

Antarctica

N
W E
S

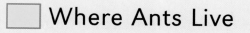 Where Ants Live

Ants in the World

Ants are found around the world. All ants live on land. Some ants are found on mountains and islands. Most ants live in tropical areas. Ants can even live in very dry areas. Silver ants live in the hot Sahara Desert.

Ants move from place to place by flying or crawling. Ants with wings fly to mate. Then they move to new places and make nests. Some ants cannot fly, so they crawl.

◀ Ants live on all continents except Antarctica.

Ant Habitats

Ants live in groups in nests. Ant nests can be underground, in wood, or inside plants. Ant nests often have many tunnels and rooms.

Ants sometimes connect many small nests to form a large nest. In Europe, ants formed a huge nest. It stretches across 3,728 miles (6,000 kilometers), from Italy to Spain.

◀ Many ants build nests after it rains. Building is easier when the soil is wet and moveable.

What Ants Eat

Some ants eat insects and animals. Ants eat beetles, termites, flies, spider eggs, and earthworms. Ants even eat other ants.

Other ants eat plants and fungi. Harvester ants gather and eat seeds. Leaf-cutting ants cut off pieces of plants. They then carry them to their nests. Later, fungi will grow on the plants. Fungi, such as mushrooms, have no leaves, flowers, or roots. Leaf-cutting ants eat the fungi.

◄ A group of ants find a dead fly. Later they will carry it back to their nest and eat it.

Life Cycle of an Ant

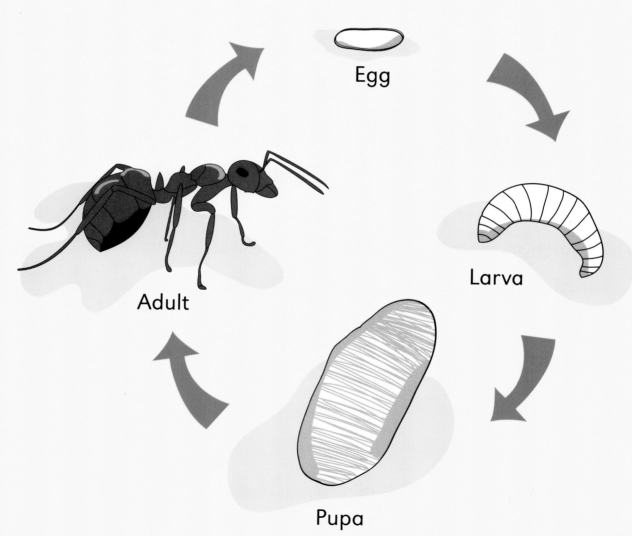

Egg

Larva

Pupa

Adult

Eggs and Larvae

Queen ants mate with males and then lay eggs. An ant changes from egg to **larva** to **pupa** to adult. Ants begin life as white, rounded eggs. Adult ants keep eggs clean.

Depending on weather, most eggs become larvae in only a few days. Larvae are white and have no eyes or legs. They grow and **molt**, shedding their exoskeleton. Some larvae make silk **cocoons** to grow in while they are pupae.

Pupae and Adults

Pupae do not eat or walk. Not all pupae grow in cocoons. Some look like white adults when they are pupae. After about two weeks, pupae become adults.

Adult ants are queens, males, or workers. Males die after mating. All workers are female and have many jobs. They work together to fix nests and find food. Soldiers are special workers that protect nests.

◄ Worker ants take care of pupae. Most pupae darken in color after they become adults.

Dangers to Ants

Many animals eat ants. Anteaters, lizards, and birds eat ants. Ants are also eaten by spiders, worms, and other insects. Some ants even eat ants from different nests.

Even though ants face many dangers, billions live in the world. They eat many insects each year. Ants also mix soil when making nests. Mixing the soil helps crops grow. Ants are an important part of the world.

◄ A crab spider grabs an ant. These spiders hide on plants and wait to catch ants.

Amazing Facts about Ants

- Ants are strong for their small size. They can carry 50 times their weight.
- People have used ant heads as stitches. After an ant would bite, people removed its body. The head remained and held the cut shut.
- Ants mark trails with chemicals from their bodies. They smell the chemicals with their antennas to travel in lines.
- Slave-maker ants take ants from other nests. They make the ants work for them.

◄ A leaf-cutting ant carries another ant on a leaf. This strong ant may carry large loads for hours.

Glossary

abdomen (AB-duh-muhn)—the end section of an insect's body

antenna (an-TEN-uh)—a feeler on an insect's head

cocoon (kuh-KOON)—a covering made of silky threads; insects make a cocoon to protect themselves while they change from larvae to pupae.

exoskeleton (eks-oh-SKE-luh-tuhn)—the hard outer covering of an insect

larva (LAR-vuh)—an insect at the stage after an egg; more than one larva are larvae.

molt (MOHLT)—to shed an outer layer of skin, or exoskeleton, so a new exoskeleton can be seen

pupa (PYOO-puh)—an insect at the stage of development between a larva and an adult; more than one pupa are pupae.

thorax (THOR-aks)—the middle section of an insect's body

Read More

Jacobs, Liza. *Ants.* Wild Wild World. San Diego: Blackbirch Press, 2003.

Ross, Edward S. *Ants.* Naturebooks. Chanhassen, Minn.: Child's World, 2003.

Internet Sites

FactHound offers a safe, fun way to find Internet sites related to this book. All of the sites on FactHound have been researched by our staff.

Here's how:
1. Visit *www.facthound.com*
2. Type in this special code **0736837051** for age-appropriate sites. Or enter a search word related to this book for a more general search.
3. Click on the **Fetch It** button.

FactHound will fetch the best sites for you!

Index